A Note From Rick Renner

I am on a personal quest to see a "revival of the Bible" so people can establish their lives on a firm foundation that will stand strong and endure the test when the end-time storm winds begin to intensify.

In order to experience a revival of the Bible in your personal life, it is important to take time each day to read, receive, and apply its truths to your life. James tells us that if we will continue in the perfect law of liberty — refusing to be forgetful hearers but determined to be doers — we will be blessed in our ways. As you watch or listen to the programs in this series and work through this corresponding study guide, I trust that you will search the Scriptures and allow the Holy Spirit to help you hear something new from God's Word that applies specifically to your life. I encourage you to be a doer of the Word that He reveals to you. Whatever the cost, I assure you — it will be worth it.

> Thy words were found, and I did eat them;
> and thy word was unto me the joy and rejoicing of mine heart:
> for I am called by thy name, O Lord God of hosts.
> — Jeremiah 15:16

Your brother and friend in Jesus Christ,

Rick Renner

How To Navigate a Pandemic and Other Coming Periods of Isolation

Copyright © 2021 by Rick Renner
8316 E. 73rd St.
Tulsa, Oklahoma 74133

Published by Rick Renner Ministries
www.renner.org

ISBN 13: 978-1-68031-859-3

eBook ISBN 13: 978-1-68031-860-9

How To Use This Study Guide

This five-lesson study guide corresponds to *"How To Navigate a Pandemic and Other Coming Periods of Isolation" With Rick Renner* (Renner TV). Each lesson in this study guide covers a topic that is addressed during the program series, with questions and references supplied to draw you deeper into your own private study of the Scriptures on this subject.

To derive the most benefit from this study guide, consider the following:

First, watch or listen to the program prior to working through the corresponding lesson in this guide. (Programs can also be viewed at **renner.org** by clicking on the Media/Archives links.)

Second, take the time to look up the scriptures included in each lesson. Prayerfully consider their application to your own life.

Third, use a journal or notebook to make note of your answers to each lesson's Study Questions and Practical Application challenges.

Fourth, invest specific time in prayer and in the Word of God to consult with the Holy Spirit. Write down the scriptures or insights He reveals to you.

Finally, take action! Whatever the Lord tells you to do according to His Word, do it.

For added insights on this subject, it is recommended that you obtain Rick Renner's books *Last-Days Survival Guide: A Scriptural Handbook To Prepare You for These Perilous Times* and *Build Your Foundation: Six Must-Have Beliefs for Constructing an Unshakable Christian Life.* You may also select from Rick's other available resources by placing your order at **renner.org** or by calling 1-800-742-5593.

TOPIC

Fill Yourself With Good Resources

SCRIPTURES

1. **Luke 21:11** — And great earthquakes shall be in divers places, and famines, and pestilences; and fearful sights and great signs shall there be from heaven.

2. **2 Timothy 4:13** — The cloke that I left at Troas with Carpus, when thou comest, bring with thee, and the books, but especially the parchments.

GREEK WORDS

1. "sign" — **σημεῖον** (*semeion*): a sign or marker you would see on the road as you were traveling to a new place; pictures a marker or sign to alert a traveler to where he is on a road

2. "pestilences" — **λοιμός** (*loimos*): plural, pestilences; old diseases being reactivated or newly emerging diseases never seen before

3. "books" — **βιβλία** (*biblia*): plural, books; scrolls; a papyrus roll; a leather parchment

SYNOPSIS

The five lessons in this study on ***How To Navigate a Pandemic and Other Coming Periods of Isolation*** will focus on the following topics:

- Fill Yourself With Good Resources
- Reach Out to Someone Else
- Connect by Technology
- Get Work Done and Wrap Up Projects
- Lose Weight and Get in Shape

The emphasis of this lesson:

When you find yourself in places of isolation, maximize your time by feeding your spirit good books and godly teachings from anointed

ministers. It will expand your spiritual capacity, renew your mind with truth, and empower you to successfully go through anything.

Pandemics Are a Major Sign of the End of the Age

Throughout human history, civilization has been hit by all kinds of plagues, including the Black Death of 1350, another pandemic of bubonic plague during the 1600s, and the Spanish flu of 1918, which caused the deaths of nearly 50 million people worldwide. The most recent pandemic, which has been labeled COVID-19, is just one more sign of the very end of the age that Jesus said we would see before He returns.

Matthew 24 captures a candid conversation between Jesus and His disciples regarding the last days. In verse 3, the Bible says, "And as he [Jesus] sat upon the mount of Olives, the disciples came unto him privately, saying, Tell us, when shall these things be? and what shall be the sign of thy coming, and of the end of the world?" Although the disciples asked for *one* sign, Jesus gave them many signs.

The word "sign" in Matthew 24:3 is the Greek word *semeion*, which was the very word used in the First Century to describe *the signs or markers you would see on the road as you were traveling to a new place.* Those signs were there to alert travelers where they were on their journey and how much further they had to go before reaching their destination. The closer we get to our destination, the more signs we see to tell us just how close we actually are to where we are headed. Once we reach our destination, a large sign usually greets us and lets us know we have arrived.

In this case, the disciples were asking, "Lord, where are we on God's prophetic timeclock? How much further do we have to go? If we're actually on the road to the end of the age, what are the authenticating markers that will confirm it?" What's interesting is that Jesus specifically said that *pandemics* are a major sign we will see as the end of the age begins to wrap up.

'Pestilences' Is the Bible's Name for Pandemics

The conversation Jesus had with His disciples on the Mount of Olives that is recorded in Matthew 24 is also captured in Luke 21. In verse 11, Jesus specifically said, "And great earthquakes shall be in divers places, and famines, and pestilences; and fearful sights and great signs shall there be from heaven."

Notice the word "pestilences." It is the Greek word *loimos*, which is plural, indicating there will be *multiple pestilences*. This word *loimos* describes *old diseases being reactivated* or *newly emerging diseases never seen before*. This lets us know that at the very end of the age, we're going to see diseases and plagues reactivated that we thought were over and done with. Likewise, we're also going to see newly emerging diseases we have never seen before begin to make an impact on the global population.

This is where we currently find ourselves in the midst of this pandemic. And according to Jesus, there are others that will follow. Therefore, we need to know how we are to respond and navigate these pandemics and other coming periods of isolation.

Feed Your Spirit Good Things

The Holy Spirit gives us insight on what we are to do in times of isolation in the book of Second Timothy. At the time the apostle Paul wrote this second letter, he was in prison in Rome awaiting his execution. It was a time of seclusion where all his ministry travels and speaking opportunities had come to an end. It was during this time Paul wrote to Timothy with this specific request: "The cloke that I left at Troas with Carpus, when thou comest, bring with thee, and the books, but especially the parchments" (2 Timothy 4:13).

In this verse, Paul asked Timothy to bring him his "books." This word is a translation of the Greek word *biblia*, which is the plural form of the word *biblion*, and it describes *books*; *scrolls*; *a papyrus roll*; or *a leather parchment*. In this passage, Paul was literally saying, "Timothy, I'm sitting in isolation and quarantined from everyone else. I have a lot of time on my hands, so I want to maximize it as best as I can. Although I can't do anything about my situation, I can fill my mind with the right things. So bring me my good books to read."

Instead of just sitting around twiddling his thumbs or trying to find ways to "kill time," Paul chose to maximize the time he had by feeding his soul and spirit good things. By doing so, he was setting his mind on things above (*see* Colossians 3:1,2) as he waited and looked forward to seeing the Lord Jesus.

The fact is, time is a precious commodity. Each day is a gift you have been given and not something you should waste. If the apostle Paul, who authored nearly two-thirds of the New Testament, needed to fill himself with good, faith-building books, we need to make every effort to do the same thing. Feeding on God's Word and Holy-Spirit inspired materials each day will powerfully strengthen your spirit. Just as fertilizer helps nourish the plants in a garden, so reading and listening to anointed teachings will nourish your spirit and renew your mind, empowering you to grow at a faster pace spiritually.

A List of Recommended Resources

In the midst of the current pandemic we're facing, a number of people are paralyzed by the "what ifs." They ask, "What if I catch the virus? What if I lose my job? What if I never get to personally visit with my loved ones again?" In the natural, all of us face doubts and fears like these. So the last thing we want to do is listen to anything that will feed these fears. Instead, we need to feed on things that will feed our faith.

To help you maximize times of quarantine and isolation and feed on good, faith-filled teachings, here is a list of recommended Bible teachers and ministries you can access online:

Kenneth Copeland Ministries (kcm.org)

Kenneth Hagin (rhema.org)

Joyce Meyer (joycemeyer.org)

Andrew Wommack (awmi.net)

Bill Winston (billwinston.org)

Keith Moore (moorelife.org)

Bob Yandian (bobyandian.org)

John Bevere (johnbevere.com)

Perry Stone (perrystone.org)

Mario Murillo (mariomurillo.org)

Beth Jones (thebasicswithbeth.com)

Tony Cooke (tonycooke.org)

Rick Renner (renner.org)

For powerful Bible teaching to strengthen your faith and discover your authority as a believer, check out the ministries of Kenneth and Gloria Copeland as well as Kenneth Hagin. To get established in the basics of the Bible, check out Beth Jones, and for a good dose of common sense for everyday Christian living, listen to Joyce Meyer.

If you're looking for in-depth teaching on what it means to live a life led by the Spirit and the vital importance of God's Word, access the resources of Andrew Wommack and Keith Moore. And for life-giving instruction on topics such as the fear of the Lord, breaking free of fear and offense, and developing a passionate relationship with Jesus, access John Bevere's teachings.

Two of the best Bible teachers who serve as a prophetic, end-time voice to the Body of Christ are Perry Stone and Mario Murillo. For line-upon-line and verse-by-verse teaching of Scripture, check out the ministries of Bill Winston and Bob Yandian. If you are in a position of church leadership, explore the resources offered by Tony Cooke. And of course, for a deeper understanding of the original Greek meaning of Scripture and how it applies to your life, continue to dive into the teachings of Rick Renner. He particularly recommends his books *Last-Days Survival Guide*; *A Life Ablaze*; *Sparkling Gems From the Greek, Volumes I and 2*; and his newest book *Build Your Foundation*.

Friend, don't attempt to survive off the fumes of yesterday's spiritual fire. Make the choice to put new fuel in the fire of your spiritual devotion to Christ. When you find yourself in places of isolation, maximize your time by feasting on good books and godly teachings from anointed ministers and ministries. It will expand your spiritual capacity, renew your mind with truth, and empower you spiritually to successfully go through anything.

In our next lesson, we will focus on the importance of reaching out to others during times of isolation and quarantine.

STUDY QUESTIONS

Study to shew thyself approved unto God, a workman that needeth not to be ashamed, rightly dividing the word of truth.
— 2 Timothy 2:15

Carefully meditate on these words of wisdom from Jesus as if He, Himself, were speaking them directly to you:

1. "...Be careful what you are hearing. The measure [of thought and study] you give [to the truth you hear] will be the measure [of virtue and knowledge] that comes back to you — and more [besides] will be given to you who hear" (Mark 4:24 *AMPC*).

   What is God showing you about the importance — and *power* — of feeding your spirit?

2. Take a few minutes to read the story in Genesis 30:32-43 of how the livestock Jacob tended was directly affected by what he placed in front of them. Symbolically, what does this story say to you about what you need to place in front of yourself in order to reproduce the character of Christ and the fruit of His Spirit in your life?

PRACTICAL APPLICATION

> But be ye doers of the word, and not hearers only,
> deceiving your own selves.
> —James 1:22

1. It is a proven fact that *readers* become *leaders*. Those who invest time reading life-giving resources are those who continue to grow spiritually. Along with the Bible, what book or books are you currently reading? Which book have you been meaning to read — or pick back up and finish — that you know you need to get into?

2. Name at least one book or study that truly revolutionized your life. In what specific ways did it change your thinking and ultimately your actions?

3. As we are working through this current pandemic and the chaotic uncertainty of what is taking place in the world, what "what-if" questions are coming against your mind trying to paralyze you? Take these thoughts and feelings to God in prayer and surrender them — and yourself — to Him! Psalm 34:4

4. What you see and hear has a powerful impact on your spiritual well-being and how you live your life. Pause for a moment and pray, *"Holy Spirit, is there anything I'm watching or listening to that is producing or feeding doubts and fears in my life? If so, what is it? Please give me the grace to turn these things off and feed on things that will feed my faith. In Jesus' name. Amen."*

TOPIC

Reach Out to Someone Else

SCRIPTURES

1. **Luke 21:11** — And great earthquakes shall be in divers places, and famines, and pestilences; and fearful sights and great signs shall there be from heaven.

2. **Hebrews 13:3** — Remember them that are in bonds, as bound with them; and them which suffer adversity, as being yourselves also in the body.

3. **James 1:27** — Pure religion and undefiled before God and the Father is this, To visit the fatherless and widows in their affliction....

4. **2 Timothy 4:13** — The cloke that I left at Troas with Carpus, when thou comest, bring with thee, and the books, but especially the parchments.

GREEK WORDS

1. "pestilences" — λοιμός (*loimos*): plural, pestilences; old diseases being reactivated or newly emerging diseases never seen before

2. "bonds" — δέσμιος (*desmios*): those who are bound; those in prison; prison was a place of terrible isolation

3. "bound with them" — συνδέω (*sundeo*): mutually bound

4. "suffer adversity" — κακουχέω (*kakoucheo*): compound of κακός (*kakos*) and ἔχω (*echo*); the word κακός (*kakos*) means evil, foul, hard, injustice; the word ἔχω (*echo*) means to have, hold, or to possess; compounded, to have a hard time, to be in a difficult or hard moment; to suffer what is perceived to be injustice

5. "visit" — ἐπισκέπτομαι (*episkeptomai*): to look upon, to physically visit, or to provide help for those in need, and it was even used to denote the provision of medical care

6. "fatherless" — ὀρφανός (*orphanos*): orphan; children left without a father or mother; used in a broader sense to describe those who felt

abandoned, deserted, forsaken, or discarded; could depict one who is deprived in some way; includes the idea of abandonment

7. "widows" — χήρα (*chera*): describes widows in the traditional sense of the word; used by Jesus in Matthew 23:14 and Luke 4:26 to describe women who were bereft of their spouses due to death

8. "affliction" — θλῖψις (*thlipsis*): great pressure; crushing pressure; a horribly tight, life-threatening squeeze; a situation so difficult it caused one to feel stressed, squeezed, pressured, or crushed

9. "especially" — μάλιστα (*malista*): most of all; especially; very much; chiefly, most of all, above all else

10. "parchments" — μεμβράνα (*membrana*): leather parchments; it was made of skin, and the first were produced in Pergamum

SYNOPSIS

Life is all about seasons. The Bible says, "To every thing there is a season, and a time to every purpose under the heaven" (Ecclesiastes 3:1). Among all the various seasons we experience, there are times we undergo periods of isolation. These include a time of quarantine from a pandemic, a sabbatical time from work or ministry, or a time of isolation to recover and regroup from personal injury or sickness. The tendency for many of us during times like these is to begin sitting around and thinking about ourselves and our situations to the point that we become extremely self-absorbed. But this is never profitable and only leads to a deeper sense of discouragement and despair. *The greatest decision we can make during a period of isolation is to get ourselves off our mind and think about someone else.*

The emphasis of this lesson:

One of the best things we can do during a pandemic is to reach out and help someone else who is struggling. Through deliberate, intentional actions, God instructs us to provide a helping hand to those who are abandoned or feel like they're afflicted and are struggling — especially the fatherless and those who are widows.

Jesus Said We Would Experience *Pandemics*

As we saw in our first lesson, the Bible says that as Jesus was sitting on the Mount of Olives with His disciples, they came to Him privately and asked Him what would be the sign of His coming and of the end of the age (*see* Matthew 24:3). We saw that the word "sign" is the Greek word *semeion*, which was the word used in the First Century to describe *the signs or markers you would see on the road as you were traveling to your destination.* These "signs" would alert a traveler of how far he or she had gone and how far that person still had to go.

Out of His great love for His disciples — both then and now — Jesus presented not just one, but numerous authenticating markers that we would see as we get closer and closer to His return for us, His Church, and to the end of age. (For a detailed overview of all these signs, check out Rick's book *Signs You'll See Just Before Jesus Comes.*)

Indeed, Jesus enumerated a long list of prophetic signs we would see that would indicate His imminent return and the end of the age. These signs are documented in Matthew 24 and Luke 21. Specifically, in Luke 21:11, Jesus said, "And great earthquakes shall be in divers places, and famines, and pestilences; and fearful sights and great signs shall there be from heaven."

We learned that the word "pestilences" in this verse is the Greek word *loimos*, which is plural, meaning there will be not one but *many pestilences* that plague humanity one after another the closer we get to the very end of the age. This word *loimos* refers to *old diseases being reactivated* or *newly emerging diseases never seen before.*

The pandemic we're experiencing right now is a tangible sign proclaiming that Jesus' return is very near! It has resulted in multitudes of people — even entire countries — being quarantined and placed in isolation. Some have even been prevented from going to church. The longer a period of isolation like this lasts, the more likely we are to become self-focused. Again, one of the best things we can do to avoid the pitfalls of self-pity and self-centeredness is to reach out and help someone else.

We Need To Remember Those Who Are in Isolation

As difficult as our situation may be, there are other people who are going through even greater challenges than we are. That is why the Bible says, "Remember them that are in bonds, as bound with them; and them which suffer adversity, as being yourselves also in the body" (Hebrews 13:3). Notice the word "bonds" in this verse. It is the Greek word *desmios*, which depicts *those who are bound* or *those in prison.* In the First Century, a Roman prison was a place of terrible isolation.

The writer of Hebrews was reminding all believers of all generations to never forget that there are others who are hurting and whose conditions are far worse than our own. We are to see ourselves as "bound with them," which in Greek is the word *sundeo*, and it means *mutually bound*. In other words, we are to imagine what it would feel like if we ourselves were in their shoes — experiencing the exact same circumstances they are experiencing.

The writer went on to say, "Remember...them which suffer adversity, as being yourselves also in the body" (Hebrews 13:3). The phrase "suffer adversity" is a translation of the Greek word *kakoucheo*, which is a compound of the words *kakos* and *echo*. The word *kakos* describes *something evil, foul,* or *hard; it indicates injustice.* And the word *echo* means *to have, to hold, or to possess.* When these words are compounded to form the word *kakoucheo*, it means *to have a hard time, to be in a difficult or hard moment*; or *to suffer what is perceived to be injustice.*

If you stop and think about it, there are many people today who feel like they've experienced a great deal of injustice. Large numbers of people have been forced to close the doors of their businesses, while others have been prohibited from going to church. There have even been some individuals who have been told they can't leave their house. They don't understand all the rules and regulations, and as a result, they just feel trapped. Regardless of who is to blame, these people are going through a very hard time, and they need our support. Hebrews 13:3 admonishes us to remember them and get our minds off ourselves.

Visit the 'Fatherless and Widows'

James, the brother of Jesus, also urged us to think about others. He said, "Pure religion and undefiled before God and the Father is this, To visit the fatherless and widows in their affliction..." (James 1:27). There are four very important words to understand the meaning of in this verse.

The first word to note is "visit." Here, it is the Greek word *episkeptomai*, which means *to look upon, to physically visit, or to provide help for those in need.* This word was even used to denote *the provision of medical care.* Hence, the word "visit" — the Greek word *episkeptomai* — denotes *deliberate, intentional actions that provide a helping hand to those who are abandoned or feel like they're afflicted and are struggling.* It is inspection, oversight, or provision that is particularly given to the fatherless and widows.

The word "fatherless" in this verse is the Greek word *orphanos*, which means *orphans*. It describes *children left without a father or mother*. In a broader sense, this word was used to describe *those who felt abandoned, deserted, forsaken, or discarded*. It could also depict *one who is deprived in some way* and includes the idea of *abandonment*. So when the Bible says to visit the fatherless, it means we are to intentionally reach out and lend a helping hand to those who are struggling with loneliness and feeling isolated and abandoned.

In addition to the fatherless, James said we are to visit "widows." In Greek, this is the word *chera*, which describes *widows in the traditional sense of the word*. It is the same word used by Jesus in Matthew 23:14 and Luke 4:26 to describe *women who were bereft of their spouses due to death*. Thus, God specifically tells us through James that we are to deliberately think about and reach out and lend a helping hand to women who have lost their spouses as a result of death.

Essentially, by using the word "widows" — the Greek word *chera* — we are being instructed to think about older people who are confined to their homes and cannot get out. If you feel like you've been trapped during the recent pandemic, just imagine how an older person who is sitting at home must feel. To some extent, they must be struggling with feelings of loneliness and abandonment. They need someone to call them and check on them — they need someone to visit them and be very intentional, providing them a helping hand to make sure they're alright.

There is one more word we need to understand in this verse, and it is the word "affliction." James said we are "…To visit the fatherless and widows in their affliction" (James 1:27). The word "affliction" here is the Greek word *thlipsis*, and it is used throughout the New Testament to describe *great pressure; crushing pressure;* or *a horribly tight, life-threatening squeeze*. This word depicts *a situation so difficult it causes one to feel stressed, squeezed, pressured, or crushed*.

To be clear, the pressures depicted through the word *thlipsis* are so great that they make it difficult to cope with life. These hardships may involve problems with housing, food, medical care, or challenges with other physical needs. Whatever the case, these struggles are so intense that they leave a person feeling hard-pressed to get up and face life on a daily basis. If we want to walk in pure religion that is undefiled in God's eyes, we must learn to get our minds off of ourselves and become involved in helping others who are struggling in this way.

Writing and Sending a Letter of Encouragement Is a Powerful Way To Express God's Love

Turning our attention once more to Second Timothy 4:13, we find the apostle Paul at the end of his life sequestered in a Roman prison writing to Timothy with this important request: "The cloke that I left at Troas with Carpus, when thou comest, bring with thee, and the books, but especially the parchments."

In addition to his books, Paul asked Timothy to especially bring the parchments. The word "especially" is the Greek word *malista*, which means *most of all; especially; very much; chiefly,* or *above all else.* And the word "parchments" in Greek is *membrane,* which is from where we get the word *membrane.* It describes *leather parchments that were made of skin,* the first of which were produced in Pergamum.

Why did Paul request these "parchments" — these *leather skins* or *membrane?* So he could write letters while he was isolated in prison. Instead of sitting and staring at the four walls of his cell or becoming self-focused and feeling sorry for himself, Paul maximized his time alone by feeding his spirit good books and writing letters of encouragement and instruction to the people and the churches he loved. Today, nearly 2,000 years later, we still have many of the letters that Paul penned while he was in jail.

Can you imagine what it was like to be many miles away and suddenly receive a hand-written letter from the apostle Paul? The truth is, if Paul would have had a mobile phone, he probably would have used it to call all the people he loved and had poured his life into. He would have utilized his time of isolation to personally check on the individuals he had led to Christ, making sure they were alright and still growing spiritually.

Aren't you glad Paul didn't sit and sulk and think to himself, *Well, no one is reaching out to check on me. I haven't received any letters while I've been in prison.* Instead, he became a mighty instrument of strength and encouragement to others. You can choose to do the same. Rather than focusing on yourself, you can make a decision to be a blessing to others. You can write people, call people, or text people a word of encouragement and hope.

Only God knows what your friends and loved ones are going through. They may be on the verge of giving up and walking away from the faith, and your phone call or text may be exactly what they need to keep them from doing something they would regret and help them continue to follow Christ.

So if you find yourself quarantined or in a time of isolation, don't see it as a setback. See it as an opportunity to be a blessing to others and seize it! When certain people's faces flood your mind, make them your personal assignment for that day. Reach out via text or phone and check on them to make sure they are alright. Ask them what you can specifically pray about for them.

Remember, what you do for others will always come back to you. It is the law of sowing and reaping (*see* Galatians 6:7-9). If you will give your time and attention to the care of others, God is bound by His Word to make sure time and attention come back to you. In our next lesson, we will focus on the value of connecting with others by technology.

STUDY QUESTIONS

Study to shew thyself approved unto God, a workman that needeth not to be ashamed, rightly dividing the word of truth.
— 2 Timothy 2:15

1. James 1:27 says that pure religion in the eyes of God the Father is to "…visit the fatherless and widows in their affliction." Do you know any children who are left without a father or mother as a result of death or even divorce? How about any widows? If so, what are their names? What could you do in the next week or two to be a blessing to these individuals?

2. When we choose to get ourselves off our mind and reach out to help others, we're choosing to walk in God's *love*. According to First John 3:17 and 18, what vital ingredient is needed for us to truly exhibit God's love?

3. Galatians 6:10 (*AMPC*) says, "…Be mindful to be a blessing, especially to those of the household of faith [those who belong to God's family with you, the believers]." When you have your mind full of ways to be a blessing to others and take action to bless them, what

can you confidently know is going to happen? (Consider Luke 6:38; Galatians 6:7,8.)

PRACTICAL APPLICATION

> But be ye doers of the word, and not hearers only,
> deceiving your own selves.
> —James 1:22

1. The Bible says, "Remember...them which suffer adversity, as being yourselves also in the body" (Hebrews 13:3). Who do you know right now that is going through a *hard time* or *difficult moment* — possibly suffering *injustice*? What specifically are they dealing with?

2. God's Word says we are to "visit" them, which in Greek means to *deliberately and intentionally provide a helping hand to those who are abandoned or feel like they're afflicted and are struggling.* Consider some practical, tangible ways you can reach out and encourage those you know who are going through a hard time — such as writing them a note, calling them on the phone, visiting them, or sending them a gift they could use. Don't put it off. Ask God to show you what to do and when to do it, and then act in faith.

3. Who did God send to "visit" you when you were going through a hard time? Briefly describe the hardship you faced and what this person did to encourage and strengthen you. Take time today to text, email, or call this person and express your appreciation for them being the hands and feet of Jesus.

LESSON 3

TOPIC

Connect by Technology

SCRIPTURES

1. **Luke 21:11** — And great earthquakes shall be in divers places, and famines, and pestilences; and fearful sights and great signs shall there be from heaven.

2. **Hebrews 10:24,25** — And let us consider one another to provoke unto love and to good works: Not forsaking the assembling of ourselves together, as the manner of some is; but exhorting one another: and so much the more, as ye see the day approaching.

GREEK WORDS

1. "pestilences" — λοιμός (*loimos*): plural, pestilences; old diseases being reactivated or newly emerging diseases never seen before

2. "consider" — κατανοέω (*katanoeo*): to thoroughly consider; to think something through from the top to the bottom; to deeply ponder; the word pictures a person engaged in focused and concentrated consideration; it is the idea of mulling something over; to carefully contemplate a matter; pondering and carefully looking at a particular issue; to contemplate

3. "provoke" — παροξυσμός (*paroxusmos*): prodding a person to do something; to incite, to inflame, or to provoke

4. "forsaking" — ἐγκαταλείπω (*egkataleipo*): pictures someone who is discouraged, defeated, and depressed; depicts one who feels left out, down, depressed, and far behind everyone else

5. "manner" — ἔθος (*ethos*): manner, custom, habit

6. "exhorting" — παρακαλέω (*parakaleo*): urge, beseech, plead, beg, pray; pictures one who has come closely alongside of another person for the sake of speaking to him, consoling him, comforting him, or assisting him with instruction, counsel, or advice; in ancient times, used to depict military leaders who came alongside their troops to urge, exhort, beseech, beg, and plead with them to stand tall and face their battles bravely

SYNOPSIS

In our first lesson, we learned that one of the best things we can do during a pandemic or a time of isolation is to feed our spirit healthy resources. That's what the apostle Paul did when he was sequestered in a Roman prison. Today, in addition to God's Word, we're blessed to have access to many great books as well as powerful teachings online that we can listen to and build our faith.

Then in Lesson 2, we saw how reaching out to check on and help others who are struggling is the best way to get our mind off of ourselves. Again, the apostle Paul modeled this for us in Second Timothy 4:13. While imprisoned, in addition to asking for books to feed his spirit, he also asked for parchments on which he could write letters to individuals he loved and the churches he had poured his life into.

The emphasis of this lesson:

Another valuable thing you can do during a pandemic or a time of isolation is to stay connected with others — in person or by technology. Instead of forsaking the assembling of ourselves together, we are to encourage and strengthen each other to stand courageously.

The Disciples Asked Jesus for a 'Sign'

As we've seen in our first two lessons, over 2,000 years ago, Jesus had a candid conversation about the end of the age with His disciples on the Mount of Olives. This is captured in Matthew 24:3, which says, "And as he [Jesus] sat upon the mount of Olives, the disciples came unto him privately, saying, Tell us, when shall these things be? and what shall be the sign of thy coming, and of the end of the world?"

The Greek word for "sign" in this verse is the word *semeion*, and it describes *a marker or sign to alert a traveler to where he is on a road*. It is an *authenticating mark* or *specific sign* that tells a person where he is and how much further he needs to go. By using this word, the disciples were asking Jesus, "What will be the specific *authenticating mark* or *markers* that will alert us to where we are on the prophetic timeline of history?"

Jesus then answered His disciples by giving them a detailed list of many signs they would see before His return and this present age wraps up. These signs are recorded in Matthew 24 as well as in Luke 21. (For a comprehensive overview of all these signs, read Rick Renner's book *Signs You'll See Just Before Jesus Comes*.)

'Pestilences' Are a Major Sign We'll See at the End of the Age

In Luke 21:11, Jesus said, "And great earthquakes shall be in divers places, and famines, and pestilences; and fearful sights and great signs shall there be from heaven." We've seen that the word "pestilences" is the Greek word *loimos*, which is plural, meaning there will be *multiple pestilences* taking place one after another. Moreover, the word *loimos* describes *old diseases being reactivated* or *newly emerging diseases never seen before.*

Clearly, what Jesus was referring to in this passage is *pandemics* and *plagues* that are going to take place with increased frequency at the end of the age. Thus, the most recent pandemic that our world has experienced is only one in a continuing series. It serves as a major sign that we are coming to the very end of the prophetic road at the end of the age.

The question is: what are we to do when pandemics of this nature strike? If you find yourself trapped inside your house for days and weeks on end, how does God want you to respond? Well, feeding your spirit a steady diet of His Word and good resources is very important. And reaching out to check on others — especially those who may feel abandoned like widows and orphans — is another great thing to do. A third directive to maximize your time is to *connect with others by technology.*

We Are To 'Consider' and 'Provoke' One Another Unto Love and Good Works

In his letter to the Ephesian believers — and believers of all generations — the apostle Paul said, "So be careful how you act; these are difficult days. Don't be fools; be wise: make the most of every opportunity you have for doing good" (Ephesians 5:15,16 *TLB*). How fitting this directive is for us today, and what a wonderful opportunity we have to connect with others through the use of technology.

The writer of Hebrews echoes this sentiment saying, "And let us consider one another to provoke unto love and to good works" (Hebrews 10:24). First of all, it is important to note that in order to consider one another, we have to be in relationship with one another. The word "consider" here is the Greek word *katanoeo*, which is a compound of the words *kata*, meaning *down*, and *noeo*, meaning *to think* or *to contemplate*. When these two words are combined to form *katanoeo*, it means *to thoroughly consider* or *to think something through from the top to the bottom*. This word depicts *deeply pondering* something and pictures *a person engaged in focused and concentrated consideration*. It is the idea of *mulling something over, to carefully contemplate a matter*, or *pondering and carefully looking at a particular issue.*

What God is saying in this verse is that as believers, we are to deeply study one another and thoroughly contemplate how we might specifically

"...provoke [one another] unto love and to good works" (Hebrews 10:24). This word "provoke" is the Greek word *paroxusmos*, which means *to prod a person to do something; to incite, to inflame, or to provoke them.*

Normally, the word *paroxusmos* carries a very negative meaning. It is used in Acts 15:39 to describe the contention that arose between Paul and Barnabas as they were getting ready to embark on their second missionary journey. The Bible says the contention was so "sharp" — which is the Greek word *paroxusmos* — that the two parted ways and chose another person to partner with them on their ministry trip.

In the case of Hebrews 10:24, the word *paroxusmos* — translated here as "provoke" — means *to prod, to incite, or provoke a person to follow the call of God and express love and do good works.* This is what the Bible says we are to "consider" — the Greek word *katanoeo*, which means we need to really put our minds to thinking about others and how we can effectively encourage and provoke them to do what is right.

A Primary Reason People Stop Going to Church Is That They Feel 'Forsaken'

The writer of Hebrews goes on to say, "Not forsaking the assembling of ourselves together, as the manner of some is; but exhorting one another: and so much the more, as ye see the day approaching" (Hebrews 10:25). What's interesting about this verse is that it reveals explicitly why so many people stop going to church.

When we look at the word "forsaking" in the original Greek, it is the word *egkataleipo*, which is a compound of three different words: *en, kata,* and *leipo.* The word *en* means *in*; the word *kata* means *down*; and the word *leipo* means *to be behind.* When these three words are compounded to form the new word *egkataleipo*, it pictures *someone who is discouraged, defeated, and depressed.* It is *one who feels left out, down, depressed, and far behind everyone else.* As a result, they just give up and quit attending church.

Sadly, the very place these hurting people need to be — in the church — they no longer go. Hence, they miss out on hearing the life-changing Word of God that would strengthen their faith, and they forego the benefits of being sharpened and encouraged by fellow believers. The truth is, many of these individuals are embarrassed because they don't have victory in their lives. In fact, they're so discouraged and defeated that they cannot bear to be around others who are speaking positive confessions. This is why it's so imperative that we get ourselves off our mind and reach out to others — especially those who feel *forsaken*.

To be clear, we need the fellowship of other believers, which is why we are not to forsake the assembling of ourselves together "…as the manner of some is…" (Hebrews 10:25). The word "manner" here is the Greek word *ethos*, and it describes *a manner, a custom, or a habit*. For some believers, not going to church has become a habit, but we can't let that be our story.

God Wants Us To 'Exhort' Each Other

Now more than ever, we need to be "…exhorting one another: and so much the more, as ye see the day approaching" (Hebrews 10:25). The word "exhorting" here is the Greek word *parakaleo*, which is a compound of the word *para*, meaning *alongside*, and the word *kaleo*, meaning *to call* or *to beckon*. When these two words are compounded to form *parakaleo*, it means *to urge, beseech, plead, beg, or pray*. It pictures *one who has come closely alongside of another person for the sake of speaking to him, consoling him, comforting him, or assisting him with instruction, counsel, or advice.*

In ancient times, the word *parakaleo* — translated here as "exhorting" — was used to depict military leaders who came alongside their troops to urge, exhort, beseech, beg, and plead with them to stand tall and face their battles bravely. By using the word *parakaleo*, it indicates that as we approach the end of the age, we need to make a practice of coming alongside one another regularly to encourage and strengthen each other to stand courageously.

So many things are going to be happening in the world and in society as the Church age wraps up, and we are going to need to speak to each other like fellow soldiers and urge one another to stand straight, hold our head high, throw our shoulders back, and face our battles bravely. God doesn't want us to give out or give in. He wants us to faithfully keep going to church.

Now, you may say, "My church is currently not having regular services, because there are all kinds of restrictions due to the pandemic. What should I do?" Good question — and connecting through technology is a great option. Today, we can actually attend church online. We can participate in worship and feed on the teaching of God's Word right from our own homes. In many cases, we can interact and offer comments, receive prayer, and give financially. The truth is, it has never been easier to invite someone to church than right now. The online church option has made a way for countless numbers of people to hear the Gospel and invite Christ into their lives to be their Lord and Savior.

Keep in mind that it is very important to guard your heart by being mindful of what you allow to enter your eyes and fill your ears. Fear-filled information has no place in you, neither does spiritual nonsense that is not founded on Scripture. Selectively decide what you're going to feed your spirit. If you're unable to physically attend your church but it has an online option, use it. If your church is closed and it doesn't have an online service, make every effort to find a healthy online church so that you can hear the life-giving Word of God and receive strength and encouragement from fellow believers.

Technology Provides Incredible Opportunities

One of the most wonderful advantages of technology is the ability to access great resources and teaching that is thousands of miles away as well as just around the corner. Amazingly, the spiritual gift that's inside of each pastor, teacher, prophet, or evangelist actually comes right into your heart through the pipeline of innovative technology. You're not just receiving from a computer; you're receiving from the Spirit of God Himself coming out of that brother or sister in Christ.

There are many wonderful pastors and churches online for you to choose from, such as Pastor Kenneth Hagin at Rhema Bible Church (**rhemabiblechurch.com**), which we previously mentioned. Additionally, we encourage you to check out the ministry of Rodney Howard-Browne (**revival.com**) as well as Eagle Mountain International Church (**emic. org**) where you can listen to Pastors George and Terri Pearsons. These are truly remarkable Bible teachers that will certainly feed your spirit and help renew your mind with good, solid, faith-filled truth. (Please refer back to Lesson 1 for the full list of recommended ministry sites.)

And by all means, if the church or ministry you are watching has a place where you can comment and participate online, do it. Take the time to encourage others — including the pastor. If possible, message others who are watching with you and pray for each other. Make the most of the situation you are facing by helping to build an online community of faith. If you're in isolation or in quarantine and can't get out, then do what you *can* do. But don't let your new *ethos* — your *custom* or *habit* — be that you no longer go to church. As God's Word says,

> **Let us not neglect our church meetings, as some people do, but encourage and warn each other, especially now that the day of his coming back is drawing near.**
>
> Hebrews 10:25 (*TLB*)

In our next lesson, we will focus on the importance of getting work done and wrapping up projects.

STUDY QUESTIONS

> **Study to shew thyself approved unto God, a workman that needeth not to be ashamed, rightly dividing the word of truth.**
> — 2 Timothy 2:15

1. Never underestimate the power of good, godly relationships! Although "…evil communications corrupt good manners" (1 Corinthians 15:33), a good friend sharpens you as "iron sharpens iron" (*see* Proverbs 27:17). According to Ecclesiastes 4:9-12, what is the value of being in a healthy relationship with others (also consider Proverbs 17:17)? Who are you doing life with that helps meet these needs?

2. As you connect by technology and search for things to feed your spirit, be mindful of what you allow to enter your eyes and ears. Fear-filled information and spiritual nonsense that's not founded on Scripture has no place in you. Take time to reflect on, write out, and commit to memory **Philippians 4:8**. Let it become your *filter* that helps you selectively decide what you're going to let in and what you're going to keep out of your thinking. (Also consider Joshua 1:8; Colossians 3:16; Second Timothy 3:16 and 17.)

PRACTICAL APPLICATION

> **But be ye doers of the word, and not hearers only, deceiving your own selves.**
> — James 1:22

1. The Bible says that as believers, we're to deeply study one another and thoroughly contemplate how we might "…provoke [one another] unto love and to good works" (Hebrews 10:24). What are some

creative ways you have used to help incite and prod others to display God's love and do good? How have others effectively prodded and incited you to do what's right?

2. Who do you know that stopped going to church because they became *discouraged, defeated, depressed*, and *felt left out and far behind everyone else*? When was the last time you prayed for this person and reached out to check on them to see how they were getting along? Take time now to pray for them and then reach out to them by phone to encourage them in the faith and see how you might help them.

3. How about you? Have you stopped going to church for any of these same reasons or for a different reason altogether? If so, what is it? What specific steps is this lesson motivating you to take to reconnect with God's people?

TOPIC

Get Work Done and Wrap Up Projects

SCRIPTURES

1. **Luke 21:11** — And great earthquakes shall be in divers places, and famines, and pestilences; and fearful sights and great signs shall there be from heaven.

2. **Proverbs 24:30-34** — I went by the field of the slothful, and by the vineyard of the man void of understanding; and, lo, it was all grown over with thorns, and nettles had covered the face thereof, and the stone wall thereof was broken down. Then I saw, and considered it well: I looked upon it, and received instruction. Yet a little sleep, a little slumber, a little folding of the hands to sleep: So shall thy poverty come as one that travelleth; and thy want as an armed man.

GREEK WORDS

1. "pestilences" — λοιμός (*loimos*): plural, pestilences; old diseases being reactivated or newly emerging diseases never seen before

SYNOPSIS

The Disciples Were Captivated
With Knowing When the End Would Be

It's been 2,000 years since Jesus' time on earth, and what's interesting is that believers then were just as fascinated with understanding end-time prophecy as believers are today. The disciples were so intrigued by knowing when the end of the age would be that they asked Jesus about it directly. The Bible says, "And as he sat upon the mount of Olives, the disciples came unto him privately, saying, Tell us, when shall these things be? and what shall be the sign of thy coming, and of the end of the world?" (Matthew 24:3)

Notice the disciples asked Jesus, "*What* shall be the sign of thy coming?" The word "what" here is a translation of the Greek word *ti*, which describes *the most minute, minuscule detail.* The use of this word lets us know that the disciples were saying, "Lord, don't be vague and leave us in the dark. Please tell us *exactly* and *explicitly* what the sign of Your coming will be."

We've seen in each of the previous lessons that the Greek word for "sign" here is *semeion*, and it describes *a marker or road sign to alert a traveler to where he is on his journey.* This word denotes *authenticating marks,* or *specific signs* that tell a person where he is — *and* how much further he needs to go to reach his destination. By using this word *semeion* — translated here as "sign" — the disciples were saying, "Lord, what's the authenticating marker we're going to see as we travel down the prophetic road that will let us know how close we are to Your coming and the end of the age? Tell us precisely, down to the most minute detail, what it is."

Just as the disciples went to Jesus privately and asked Him for answers to their questions, you too can go to Jesus in prayer and ask Him for answers to your questions. James 1:5 (*NKJV*) says, "If any of you lacks wisdom, let him ask of God, who gives to all liberally and without reproach, and it will be given to him." Friend, when you draw near to God, He will draw near to you (*see* James 4:8). As you sincerely seek Him for wisdom and direction, He will open His hand and His heart and share with you what you need to know.

The emphasis of this lesson:

Inactivity and laziness produce disastrous consequences. This principle is made most clear in the book of Proverbs. Thus, it is in your best interest to rise up and take action while you have the chance. Downtime during a pandemic or time of isolation is a valuable gift from God to help you get work done and wrap up projects.

Recapping Three Practical Ways To Maximize Moments of Isolation

The conversation Jesus had with His disciples on the Mount of Olives that is recorded in Matthew 24 is also in Luke 21. Speaking prophetically about what would take place at the very end of the age, Jesus said, "And great earthquakes shall be in divers places, and famines, and pestilences; and fearful sights and great signs shall there be from heaven" (Luke 21:11)

Along with cataclysmic seismic activity and widespread famines, Jesus said there would be "pestilences." In Greek, this is the word *loimos*, which is plural, meaning *many pestilences*. It describes *old diseases being reactivated*, which indicates we're going to see some diseases we thought were defeated and long gone make a comeback. Furthermore, the word *loimos* — translated here as "pestilences" — also denotes *newly emerging diseases never seen before*. Thus, Jesus prophesied that before He returns and the present age wraps up, society is going to experience pandemics one after the other.

This is why we need to know what the Bible says about walking in divine health and experiencing supernatural healing. This includes God's powerful words through the apostle John, "Beloved, I wish above all things that thou mayest prosper and be in health, even as thy soul prospereth" (3 John 2). In these last of the last days, we also need to know how to exercise our authority as believers as well as how to cast out demons. It is only through the supernatural wisdom of God's Word and the power of His Holy Spirit that we will be able to successfully navigate these perilous times.

In the midst of the coming and going of various pestilences, sickness and disease will place many people into periods of quarantine and isolation. We have seen this firsthand in our time, and more periods of isolation are coming. The question is: what are we to do during such times? So far, we have talked about three biblical responses to navigating a pandemic and times of isolation:

1. Fill your spirit with good resources (*see* Lesson 1).
2. Get your mind off of yourself and reach out to someone else (*see* Lesson 2).
3. Connect by technology with others — including your church if you are unable to attend in person (*see* Lesson 3).

What else can you do to maximize your time during periods of isolation? You can seize the moments you're given *to get work done and wrap up projects*. Let's face it, when you're confined to your house with nowhere to go, all of your surroundings begin to stare you in the face. You're confronted with cluttered closets, disorganized bedrooms, and messy living spaces. Like many, you probably have a great deal of worthless things piled up in your garage, and your lawn and gardens are in desperate need of tending. If procrastination or lack of free time has taken its toll on your home, isn't it time you did something about it?

A Powerful Portrait of What Laziness Produces

There are a number of passages in Scripture that reveal the consequences of an undisciplined life, but few paint a more vivid picture than Proverbs 24:30-34. Consider these words of wisdom from King Solomon:

> **I went by the field of the slothful, and by the vineyard of the man void of understanding; and, lo, it was all grown over with thorns, and nettles had covered the face thereof, and the stone wall thereof was broken down (Proverbs 24:30,31).**

A person who is slothful is one who is inactive, apathetic, and in some cases lazy. What are the results of living a life of such idleness? The Bible says it produces a life that is overgrown with thorns and nettles. In other words, a slothful person becomes overwhelmed with aggravating, irritating issues that are difficult to deal with. In fact, because they haven't taken care of things, their life — including their home — is falling to pieces. The Bible goes on to say:

> **Then I saw, and considered it well: I looked upon it, and received instruction. Yet a little sleep, a little slumber, a little folding of the hands to sleep: so shall thy poverty come as one that travelleth; and thy want as an armed man (Proverbs 24:32-34).**

Basically, this verse tells us that sitting around twiddling one's thumbs and sleeping as long as one wants is a recipe for poverty. And when it arrives, it's going to show up suddenly and be overwhelming. In order to avoid the disastrous consequences of inactivity and laziness, it is in your best interest to rise up and take action now while you have the chance.

Rick candidly shared how many years ago when he and Denise were still living in the United States, they were living in a beautiful neighborhood in Tulsa, Oklahoma. During that time, he was traveling extensively all across the nation, preaching and teaching the Word. Sadly, he neglected the care of his lawn and yard, and it became quite an eyesore in the community. In fact, Rick's yard was so deplorable that the garden club officials of his neighborhood wrote him a letter expressing their frustrations. Embarrassed and humiliated by their cutting words, Rick took immediate action and cleaned things up, and he never allowed his home to fall in disrepair again.

How About You?

What is confronting you at your house? Is it your garage that is jammed with junk or your closets crammed with clutter? Is it overgrown gardens and shrubs? Is it faded and peeling wallpaper in the kitchen or bathroom? Is it broken floor tiles or carpet that needs to be cleaned? If you've been saying, "I'll get around to it one of these days," one of these days has arrived! Whatever is staring you in the face, seize the opportunity this season of isolation has provided and catch up on some projects that really need to get done.

To help you prioritize things, take a walk through your home and around the outside of your house and make a list of what needs to be done. If you're married, take your spouse along with you. Once you've jotted everything down, place the projects in order of priority and make a decision to begin getting things done by the time the season of isolation is over.

Now maybe your house is already organized and in order and your yard looks like a picture in a magazine. If so, that's wonderful. Maybe this season of isolation is an opportunity for you to write that book God put in your heart or begin developing your singing voice or maybe get your finances in order. Although God didn't send the pandemic, He will certainly use it for your good if you let Him. All you have to do is do your part and seize the opportunity set before you. He will give you the wisdom, creativity, and strength to complete the task.

Friend, don't let this season of isolation go by and everything in your home — and life — stay the same. Make the most of the opportunity! Seize the moment to upgrade your living space. As you step up and do what you know you need to do, you will also receive a sense of accomplishment and dignity for tackling something you were convicted about doing. And more important, you will experience a sense of peace in your heart and mind that is truly life-giving.

In our final lesson, we will focus on one more very important thing you can do to make the most of a pandemic and times of isolation, and that is to lose weight and get in shape.

STUDY QUESTIONS

Study to shew thyself approved unto God, a workman that needeth not to be ashamed, rightly dividing the word of truth.
— 2 Timothy 2:15

1. Carefully reread Proverbs 24:30-34. What is the Holy Spirit speaking to you personally through this passage? Are there any actions steps you sense Him asking you to take to avoid the consequences of inactivity? If so, what are they?

2. Although many people cringe at the sound of the word "discipline," it's actually one of the most rewarding principles in life. According to Hebrews 12:5-13:

   • How does God want you to *view* discipline?

   • How does He want you to *respond* to discipline?

   • What are the amazing *benefits* of discipline?

Also consider Deuteronomy 8:5; Proverbs 3:11,12; Revelation 3:19.

PRACTICAL APPLICATION

But be ye doers of the word, and not hearers only, deceiving your own selves.
—James 1:22

1. Just as the disciples went to Jesus privately and asked Him for answers to their questions, you, too, can go to Jesus and ask Him for answers to *your* questions. What concerns are currently weighing you down? Take them to God right now in prayer. He wants you to feel free to pour out your heart to Him any time (*see* Psalm 62:8) and to cast your cares upon Him because He cares for you greatly (*see* 1 Peter 5:7).

2. Of all of your areas in your home, name the top three that are staring you in the face that you know you really need to organize and clean. Place each of these areas individually on a specific day of your calendar. When that day comes, begin to go through things — boxing up what you can give to charity and throwing away what is useless.

3. If your home is already organized and in great condition, there is likely something else God wants you to focus on — something you've been putting off that He really needs you to get done. What might that be? And what practical steps can you take to obediently carry out what He has asked you to do?

LESSON 5

TOPIC

Lose Weight and Get in Shape

SCRIPTURES

1. **Luke 21:11** — And great earthquakes shall be in divers places, and famines, and pestilences; and fearful sights and great signs shall there be from heaven.

2. **1 Corinthians 6:19** — What? know ye not that your body is the temple of the Holy Ghost which is in you, which ye have of God, and ye are not your own?

3. **1 Timothy 4:8** — For bodily exercise profits little, but godliness is profitable for all things, having promise of the life that now is and of that which is to come.

4. **1 Thessalonians 4:4** — That every one of you should know how to possess his vessel in sanctification and honour.

5. **Proverbs 23:2** — And put a knife to thy throat, if thou be a man given to appetite.

6. **1 Corinthians 10:31** — Whether therefore ye eat, or drink, or whatsoever ye do, do all to the glory of God.

GREEK WORDS

1. "pestilences" — **λοιμός** (*loimos*): plural, pestilences; old diseases being reactivated or newly emerging diseases never seen before

2. "temple" — **ναός** (*naos*): a temple or a highly decorated shrine; the image of vaulted ceilings, marble, granite, gold, silver, and highly decorated ornamentation; the most sacred, innermost part of a temple; the Holy of Holies

3. "bodily exercise" — **σωματικὴ γυμνασία** (*somatike gumnasia*): **σῶμα** (*soma*) means body and **γυμνασία** (*gumnasia*) means exercise; **γυμνασία** is derived from **γυμνάζω** (*gumnadzo*), which is used to portray naked athletes who exercised, trained, and prepared for competition in the athletic games of the ancient world; removing one's clothes was necessary to eliminate all hindrances that otherwise could impede an athlete's movements; the ancient world believed discipline of the body was one of life's chief concerns and that it was essential for physical, mental, and spiritual advancement

4. "profits" — **ὠφέλιμος** (*opheilimos*): to be morally obligated; to do something as an obligation; to be indebted; it originally was a legal term to depict one's duty to fulfill obligations; used in this context, it means one has an absolute duty to exercise

5. "little" — **ὀλίγος** (*oligos*): small; few; little; is short-lived; though necessary, it is temporal

6. "possess" — **κτάομαι** (*ktaomai*): control; manage; possess; to win the mastery over

7. "vessel" — **σκεῦος** (*skeuos*): a vessel to contain something; a household utensil; any instrument by which anything is done; a household utensil; a tent

8. "honor" — **τιμή** (*time*): valuable; of great worth; honorable; something that has value in the eyes of the beholder; precious

SYNOPSIS

As we travel through life, there are several different kinds of isolation we experience. Sometimes it is the result of a pandemic, and other times it is the result of changes in our lives, such as moving into a new community, changing jobs, changing churches, or a change in our relationships. Likewise, there are times people feel isolated when they take a much needed sabbatical from work or even when they're on vacation. Rather than just sit around staring into space or twiddling our thumbs, there are things we can do to constructively maximize the time. So far, we have examined four specific activities. These include:

1. Filling your spirit with good resources (*see* Lesson 1).
2. Getting yourself off of your mind by reaching out to others who are struggling (*see* Lesson 2).
3. Connecting by technology. If you can't physically go to church, attend online (*see* Lesson 3).
4. Wrapping up projects around your house (*see* Lesson 4).

The emphasis of this lesson:

Another valuable way to make the most of a pandemic or period of isolation is to lose weight and get in shape. Your body is the temple of the Holy Spirit, and God wants you to learn how to treat it as a special container of His presence — managing it in an honorable way. Physical exercise is an important ingredient to taking care of God's temple.

A Review of Our Anchor Verse

One day, after leaving the temple area in Jerusalem, Jesus and His disciples made their way to the Mount of Olives. And the Bible says, "And as he [Jesus] sat upon the mount of Olives, the disciples came unto him privately, saying, Tell us, when shall these things be? and what shall be the sign of thy coming, and of the end of the world?" (Matthew 24:3) There are five key words in this verse.

First is the word **"when."** It is the Greek word *pote*, and it describes *specific information* and pictures *one seeking a concrete answer.* The disciples asked Jesus for very *specific, concrete information* regarding when the things that He had spoken of would take place.

Second is the word **"what."** In Greek, it is the word *ti*, which describes *a minute, minuscule detail.* The use of this word lets us know that the disciples were saying, "Lord, don't be vague. Tell us *precisely*, down to the smallest detail, what the sign of Your coming will be."

Next is the word **"sign."** It is the Greek word *semeion*, and it describes *a marker or sign to alert a traveler to where he is on a road*. This was an *authenticating mark* or *specific sign* letting one know how far he had traveled and how much further he had to go to reach his destination. By using the word *semeion*, the disciples were saying, "Lord, tell us *precisely* what signs we're going to see as we travel down the prophetic road to the end of the world. What will be the *markers* that tell us where we are prophetically and alert us to how much further we have to go before You return?"

The word **"world"** here is actually a poor translation. In Greek, it is the word *aionos*, and it describes *an age*. The disciples understood that the current age would eventually run its course and come to an end and give birth to another age. We know from Scripture that the next age will be the Great Tribulation.

The fifth word to note is the word **"end."** It is the Greek word *sunteleias*, and it describes *the closure, summation, or wrap-up of something*. The inclusion of this word is the equivalent of the disciples saying, "Lord, tell us *exactly* and *specifically* when all these things will be. What will be the *authenticating road markers* to tell us where we are prophetically? And what will be the sign that this current age is about to wrap up?"

'Pestilences' Will Abound
As We Approach the End of the Age

We have noted that this conversation between Jesus and His disciples regarding the end of the age is recorded in Matthew 24 as well as Luke 21. If you want to know all the signs Jesus said we would see before His return and the end of the age, you'll find them in these chapters. (And for an in-depth description of all these signs, check out Rick's book *Signs You'll See Just Before Jesus Comes*.)

In Luke 21:11, Jesus gave us one specific sign that confirms what we have recently been experiencing. He said, "And great earthquakes shall be in divers places, and famines, and pestilences; and fearful sights and great signs shall there be from heaven" (Luke 21:11). We have noted that the word "pestilences" is the Greek word *loimos*, and in this verse it is plural, indicating *many pestilences*. Although there were "pestilences" during the First Century, Jesus was not speaking about His time. He was prophetically pointing His finger 2,000 years into the future — to our time — and saying there shall be many "pestilences" at the wrap up or very end of the age.

This word *loimos* — translated here as "pestilences" — describes *old diseases that have had new life breathed into them and they've become reactivated.* At the same time, it also describes *newly emerging diseases never seen before* that make an impact on the population globally, which is why we call it a *pandemic.* In other words, what we have come through recently is what we're going to face again in the future.

What results from a pandemic? Periods of isolation in which people become confined to their homes with very restricted movement. In addition to feeding your spirit good resources, reaching out to people in need, connecting with others by technology, and finishing up projects around your house, times of isolation are also a great opportunity to lose weight and get in shape.

Your Body Is God's Temple

When you find yourself detained in your home, you are left with two basic options: You can sit around and watch TV and mindlessly eat whatever you want, which will result in poor health and excessive weight gain. *Or* you can make a daily decision to stay active, watch what you eat, and get in shape. When the pandemic is over, you'll either come out heavier than you've ever been or healthier than you've ever been. The choice is yours.

That said, it is imperative for us to always keep in mind what the apostle Paul wrote in First Corinthians 6:19: "What? know ye not that your body is the temple of the Holy Ghost which is in you, which ye have of God, and ye are not your own?"

In the *King James Version*, this verse begins with the word "what," which in Greek is an exclamation. Paul was so stunned by the behavior taking place among the believers in Corinth that he began by saying, "What! What is this?" He then added the phrase, "Know ye not." In Greek, it is the words *ouk oidate.* The word *ouk* is *an emphatic no,* and the word *oidate* is from the word *oida,* which means *to see, perceive, understand, or comprehend.* When you put these words together, it is the equivalent of Paul saying, "What's this? Do you really not get it? Have you not yet understood who you are? Do you not realize that your body is the temple of the Holy Ghost?"

The word "body" here is the Greek word *soma*, which describes the *physical body*. Paul told the Corinthian believers — *and us* — that our physical body is the temple of the Holy Spirit. The word "temple" is the Greek word *naos*, which is the term for *a temple* or *a highly decorated shrine*. It is the image of vaulted ceilings, marble, granite, gold, silver, and highly decorated ornamentation. It is the same word used in the Old Testament Septuagint to describe *the most sacred, innermost part of a temple; the Holy of Holies*.

Paul fully understood the meaning of the word *naos* (temple) and so did the Greek believers he wrote to. If you could peer into the spirit realm and see what you look like on the inside, you would be astonished by the inner beauty the Holy Spirit has fashioned within you. Internally, you are adorned with the fruit of the Spirit, the gifts of the Spirit, the righteousness of Christ, and all that He has secured for us through His death, burial, and resurrection. You're a walking, talking sanctuary of God!

And because your body is a temple of the Holy Spirit, Paul said, "…Ye are not your own" (1 Corinthians 6:19). Therefore, since we are not our own, we don't have the right to do whatever we want to with our body. We have to learn to manage our body in such a way that is profitable and pleasing to the Lord.

Physical Exercise Is Essential for Physical, Mental, and Spiritual Advancement

Many Christians today believe physical exercise is not important, and they base their claim on First Timothy 4:8, which says, "For bodily exercise profits little, but godliness is profitable for all things, having promise of the life that now is and of that which is to come." Although it appears this verse is downplaying the value of exercise, it actually does not. A closer look at some key words reveals this.

Take for example the words "bodily exercise," which is the Greek phrase *somatike gumnasia*. It is a compound of the word *soma*, which is the same word for the *physical body* that we saw in First Corinthians 6:19; and the word *gumnasia*, which means *exercise* and is from where we get the word *gymnasium*. The word *gumnasia* is derived from the Greek word *gumnadzo*, which was used to portray *naked athletes who exercised, trained, and prepared for competition in the athletic games of the ancient world*.

As strange as it may seem, removing one's clothes was necessary to eliminate all hindrances that otherwise could impede an athlete's movements. Therefore, the use of the word *gumnasia* — translated here as "exercise" — carries the idea of *removing laziness, sluggishness, all excuses, and anything else that would hinder physical movement*. Furthermore, people in the ancient world believed discipline of the body was one of life's chief concerns, and that it was essential for physical, mental, and even spiritual advancement.

The fact is, if you can control your body — which includes the cravings of taste connected with your tongue — you can control just about everything else in your life (*see* James 3:2). Believers who have learned how to master their physical bodies are those who are able to really advance spiritually.

You Have a Moral Obligation To Exercise

Now you may be thinking, *Then why did Paul say that bodily exercise profits little?* To answer that question, we need to know the meaning of the words "profits" and "little." In Greek, the word "profits" is *opheilimos*, which means *to be morally obligated; to do something as an obligation;* or *to be indebted*. It originally was a legal term to depict one's duty to fulfill obligations. In the context of this verse, it means *we have an absolute duty to exercise*.

This brings us to the word "little," which is the Greek word *oligos*, and while it means *small, few,* or *little*, it actually describes *something that is short-lived*. Though it is necessary, it is temporal. The use of this word tells us that the effects of physical exercise are short-lived and primarily affect life right now; though it is necessary, it is temporal. In contrast, godliness — which is spiritual exercise — affects our lives now and for eternity.

To be clear, the Holy Spirit speaking through the apostle Paul in First Timothy 4:8 says that **we have a moral obligation and an absolute duty to physically exercise — even though it is only profitable in this temporal life.** When we make a decision to discipline ourselves and strip off laziness and all excuses and develop our physical body through exercise, we will also develop ourselves mentally and really begin to spiritually advance.

God Calls You To Manage and Control Your Body

What else does the Bible say about the body and getting in shape? First Thessalonians 4:4 says, "That every one of you should know how to possess his vessel in sanctification and honour." The word "possess" in this verse is the Greek word *ktaomai*, which means *to control*; *to manage*; *to possess*; or *to win the mastery over*. The word "vessel" is the Greek word *skeuos*, and it describes *the human body as a vessel to contain something*. It was also used to depict *a household utensil* or *any instrument by which anything is done*.

Interestingly, the word *skeuos* — translated here as "vessel" — was also the word for *a tent*, which is a temporary, mobile dwelling place. This meaning helps us understand how our physical body is the temple of the Holy Spirit (*see* 1 Corinthians 6:19). We are containers of the very Person of God. We are mobile sanctuaries that carry within us the precious Holy Spirit everywhere we go. With that in mind, God calls on each of us to learn how to "…possess his vessel in sanctification and honour" (1 Thessalonians 4:4).

The word "sanctification" here is the Greek word *hagiasmos*, which means *complete separation*; *holy in practice*. It is taken from the word *hagios*, which describes *something that is set apart*; *consecrated*; *holy*. This tells us that our bodies are special and should be treated in a special way. They are consecrated and set apart for God's use and should be controlled in "honor." This word "honor" is the Greek word *time*, which describes *something valuable*; *of great worth*; or *honorable*.

In God's eyes, your body is something that is *precious* and exceedingly valuable. If God sees your body as valuable, shouldn't you? You are His home. And since His Spirit lives within you, He wants you to learn how to manage and control your physical body.

Do Everything to the Glory of God

As we wrap up this lesson, there is one more scripture we need to look at, and it is First Corinthians 10:31, which says, "Whether therefore ye eat, or drink, or whatsoever ye do, do all to the glory of God." This is a powerful verse that can be applied to everything we do in life. It's interesting that the Holy Spirit prompted the apostle Paul to specifically name eating and drinking in this verse. This gives us a test we can apply to *what* we take in and *how much* we take in.

When you eat or drink, ask yourself:

> *Can I keep eating and drinking like I am right now to the glory of God?*
> *Can I overeat to the glory of God?*
> *Can I be a glutton to the glory of God?*

One additional question you can ask yourself is:

Can I continue to ignore the care of my physical body and bring God glory?

Remember, your body is the temple of the Holy Spirit and you are not your own (*see* 1 Corinthians 6:19). "You were bought with a price [purchased with a preciousness and paid for, made His own]. So then, honor God *and* bring glory to Him in your body" (1 Corinthians 6:20 *AMPC*). Friend, you are morally obligated and it is your God-given duty to exercise and take care of your physical body — even though it is short-lived and primarily affects life right now.

If you want to do your very best to take care of the "temple" God has given you, take a moment to pray this prayer from your heart:

"Father, thank You for opening my eyes to the truths in this lesson. Please forgive me for neglecting the care of my body. Please show me what changes I need to begin making in what I eat and drink. Help me set a realistic goal of what my weight should be and how much weight I should lose. Help me develop a doable exercise program and eating plan, and give me the grace to discipline myself daily to achieve it. I want to bring You glory in everything I do — including my eating, drinking, and exercise. In Jesus' name. Amen!"

STUDY QUESTIONS

Study to shew thyself approved unto God, a workman that needeth not to be ashamed, rightly dividing the word of truth.
— 2 Timothy 2:15

Did you know that your physical body is the temple of the Holy Spirit? God declares this repeatedly in His Word, including verses like First Corinthians 3:16 and 6:19; Second Corinthians 6:16; and Ephesians 2:19-22. Carefully reflect on God's words through Paul in Second Corinthians 6:14-18 — in a few different versions.

1. In your own words, describe what it means to be the *temple* of the Holy Spirit.
2. What is the Holy Spirit speaking to you personally in this passage?
3. Are there any *people* or *things* God is urging you to separate from? If so, what are they?

PRACTICAL APPLICATION

> But be ye doers of the word, and not hearers only,
> deceiving your own selves.
> — James 1:22

1. Sometimes we wonder if certain things are *good* or *not good* for us to do. Is there anything in your life that falls into this category? Carefully reflect on these two related passages.

   "Everything is permissible (allowable and lawful) for me; but not all things are helpful (good for me to do, expedient and profitable when considered with other things). Everything is lawful for me, but I will not become the slave of anything or be brought under its power."
   — 1 Corinthians 6:12 (*AMPC*)

   "All things are legitimate [permissible — and we are free to do anything we please], but not all things are helpful (expedient, profitable, and wholesome). All things are legitimate, but not all things are constructive [to character] and edifying [to spiritual life]."
   — 1 Corinthians 10:23 (*AMPC*)

   Now apply these truths to the things you have questions about. What is the Holy Spirit showing you to do?

2. Each one of us is extremely unique. God has a unique plan designed just for you to help you gain and maintain optimum physical health. Take time now to seek His presence and pray the prayer at the end of this lesson. Listen and write down what the Holy Spirit reveals. Remember, the steps your take to discipline your body will position you to begin advancing physically, mentally, and even spiritually.

Notes

_____

_____

_____

_____

_____

_____

_____

_____

_____

_____

_____

_____

_____

_____

_____

_____

_____

_____

_____

_____

_____

_____

_____

_____

_____

_____

_____

_____

_____

_____

_____

Notes

Notes

Notes

Notes

Notes